FINANCIAL FREEDOM
How to Manage Your Money Wisely

JUNE HUNT

HENDRICKSON PUBLISHERS ROSE PUBLISHING

Financial Freedom: How to Manage Your Money Wisely
Copyright © 2014 Hope For The Heart
Aspire Press is an imprint of
Rose Publishing, LLC
P.O. Box 3473
Peabody, Massachusetts 01961-3473 USA
www.hendricksonrose.com

The views and opinions expressed in this book are those of
the author(s) and do not necessarily express the views of Rose
Publishing, nor is this book intended to be a substitute for mental
health treatment or professional counseling.

The information in this resource is intended as guidelines for
healthy living. Please consult qualified medical, legal, pastoral, and
psychological professionals regarding individual concerns.

For more information on Hope For The Heart, visit
www.hopefortheheart.org or call 1-800-488-HOPE (4673).

Printed in the United States of America

December 2017, 5th printing

CONTENTS

𝒟ear Friend,

Many years ago, my mother's administrative assistant, Vicki, came to me in a state of downright despair. "I'm in debt way over my head," she confided, "and I don't see any way out."

I soon learned that she owed thousands of dollars to numerous creditors (doctors, credit cards, personal loans, etc.), but her income barely covered her living expenses. Like so many others, Vicki was living paycheck to paycheck, feeling trapped and fearful. "I never thought I'd be in such a financial mess," she lamented, "and it's getting worse!"

As Vicki and I met together to review her financial picture, it didn't take long to see that her spending was out of control. Clearly, she could have been the poster child for the old saying, "If your outgo exceeds your income, your upkeep will be your downfall!"

Obviously, Vicki needed a strategy—a strategic plan for her spending, saving, and giving that would include a debt reduction plan. So together, we tailor-made a personalized plan and Vicki committed to following it.

We began by setting up a budget in writing. She needed to see why her outgo had to be *less* than her income if she sincerely wanted to get out of debt and stay out.

- First, we listed all her *sources of income* (she had only her salary).

- Next, we listed her *fixed expenses*—monthly and yearly (apartment rent, car payment, insurance, etc.).
- Then, we addressed her *discretionary spending* (food, clothing, toiletries, and entertainment).

We listed each creditor and exactly how much she owed each one.

Finally, we worked out a monthly payment plan for each regular expense and each creditor.

It was not easy for her to completely change her money habits, and it didn't happen overnight. But by faith, she persevered, and by leaning on the Lord, she gained self-control. *Within 18 months, the debt Vicki thought she'd be yoked to for life was paid in full!*

What joy she experienced that day—and what insight. You see, Vicki learned firsthand that God not only *promises* to meet our needs, but He also *does* it! The Bible says, *"My God will meet all your needs according to the riches of his glory in Christ Jesus"* (Philippians 4:19).

Today, if you feel hopeless about your finances, you may have unconsciously distanced yourself from God. Your daily anxiety is a far cry from the peacefulness the Lord has promised you. But take hope! You *can* get your finances under control! You *can* break the monthly dilemma of debt! If you apply the practical principles in this little book, you will take a big first step in that direction.

By following the biblical wisdom contained within these pages—setting clear goals and boundaries for spending, saving, and sharing—you will *keep money from being your master*. In turn, you will experience the peace that comes from allowing the Lord to be your Master—including the Master over your money.

Matthew 6:24 explains why we must allow the Lord to be our Master: *"No one can serve two masters. Either you will hate the one and love the other, or you will be devoted to the one and despise the other. You cannot serve both God and money."*

Money can be used for great good to further the Lord's work here on earth. God wants to help us discern how to spend, save, and share for the greater good of both ourselves and others.

Guided by the biblical, practical advice in these pages, you'll find helpful tools to examine what you've earned and where it went.

In the process, if you see credit card debt and overspending, please don't look away! Facing the truth about your finances is not only a matter of responsibility; it is a matter of spiritual faith. God wants you to put your total faith in Him by living according to His financial principles and by letting Him meet your needs.

For some reading these words, God is leading you to mentor a friend who is burdened with money problems. If that is you, praise God! The sample budget, scriptural wisdom, and page after page of practical tips in this book will help you guide others on a path of responsible stewardship.

Whether you need help achieving financial freedom yourself or you are helping others pursue their goals, my prayer is that you will experience the peace that comes from loving the Lord more than all earthly things. As a result, you will reflect His will for your life as you prayerfully spend, save, and share what you have.

Yours in the Lord's hope,

June Hunt

FINANCIAL FREEDOM

How to Manage Your Money Wisely

Do you struggle with managing money? Do you never seem to have enough to make ends meet? Do you secretly envy the financial wealth of others?

Whether you have a great deal of money or very little, until you really believe that the money in your possession is not *your* money but *God's* money, your finances will likely always be a source of *discontentment*.

Our heavenly Father owns it all, yet we worry and fret over not having enough. We manipulate to get more, then agonize over losing what we have.

Freedom from this preoccupation with money (financial bondage) involves more than having enough money to bask in the comfort of a prosperous lifestyle. It's more than learning to budget expenses, to save regularly, to invest wisely. True financial freedom is being **content** with what God gives you. *And contentment is a matter of the heart!*

"Keep your lives free from the love of money and be content with what you have ... "
(Hebrews 13:5)

9

DEFINITIONS

In the wee hours of the morning, Jimmy Groves stacks chairs at Madison Square Garden in New York City.

He doesn't have a dime on him, but pressed against the fold of his pocket could be his ticket out of the graveyard shift as well as out of the projects. *Mega Millions*. It's a weary laborer's dream to win the popular multi-state lottery—to turn a favorite hobby into an occupation or even permanent retirement. Jimmy has been purchasing Mega Millions lottery tickets since 2002 when the game began, and on this day his prospects for winning are as astronomical as ever.

What are the odds Jimmy faces? About 1 in 176 million.[1]

King Solomon, the wisest man who ever lived, observed ...

**"The race is not to the swift
or the battle to the strong,
nor does food come to the wise or wealth to
the brilliant or favor to the learned;
but time and chance happen to them all."
(Ecclesiastes 9:11)**

When the winning number is announced, Jimmy can't believe his ears, nor can he believe what he holds in his hands. His eyes stay glued to the nine-digit number before him: 1-17-31-37-54—one of two winning tickets. He will split the $336 million jackpot with a California man. Jimmy wins not only the lottery, he latches on to the second-biggest prize in the history of the game.

Typically, lottery winners first experience disbelief and then exhilaration at the realization that their lives will never be the same. Or will they?

The harsh reality is that 70% of all lottery winners squander their winnings in a few years, signaling that sudden wealth can lead to substantial woes. Not only are bank accounts depleted, family relationships and friendships can be irrevocably harmed.[2]

Just after winning the lottery, Jimmy already feels the pull on his wallet as he arrives home from work each morning to field about 40 calls from people—some he knows and some he doesn't know—all wanting one thing: a piece of the prize. "It's a dream turned into a nightmare," Jimmy describes. "Winning is the beginning. Living with it is pure hell."[3]

A financial windfall can easily disappear with the changing winds.

> "Cast but a glance at riches, and they are gone, for they will surely sprout wings and fly off to the sky like an eagle."
> (Proverbs 23:5)

Four Financial Myths and Truths

These major financial myths have led and will continue to lead many astray unless these beliefs are replaced with major financial truths.

#1 FINANCE

Finance is a system of money management that includes banking, circulation, credit, investments, economics, and accounting.[4]

Myth:

"If you live a godly, Christian life, you will experience financial gain and prosperity."

Truth:

According to God's Word, godliness is not a means to financial gain. The Bible calls this *"a different doctrine"* taught by false teachers.

"If anyone teaches a different doctrine. ... He has an unhealthy craving for controversy and for quarrels about words, which produce envy ... and constant friction among people who are depraved in mind and deprived of the truth, imagining that godliness is a means of gain" (1 Timothy 6:3–5 ESV).

#2 Money

Money is any means of exchange, including coins and paper currency, circulating in the culture issued by a civil authority as a measure of value.[5]

Myth:

"Money is the root of all evil."

Truth:

No, money can be used for great good. According to the Bible, it is the *"love of money"* that is *a* root of evil.

"The love of money is a root of all kinds of evil. Some people, eager for money, have wandered from the faith and pierced themselves with many griefs" (1 Timothy 6:10).

#3 Steward

A steward is a trustee, guardian, or overseer who manages the property or financial affairs of another person.[6] All creation belongs to God, and we are only stewards of His resources.

"The earth is the LORD's, and everything in it ... " (Psalm 24:1).

Myth:

"If I ever have enough money and earthly possessions, I will be happy."

Truth:

Happiness does not spring from your financial situation nor does it come from possessions or the amount of money you have, but from faithfully and wisely managing what has been entrusted to you.

"His master replied, 'Well done, good and faithful servant! You have been faithful with a few things; I will put you in charge of many things. Come and share your master's happiness!'" (Matthew 25:23).

(Read the parable of the talents in Matthew 25:14–30.)

#4 Debt

Debt is the condition of owing something to another.[7] The debtor (the one who owes another) is under obligation to pay the debt.

Myth:

"You must borrow money from a bank and pay it back in order to prove financial responsibility and to establish good credit references."

Truth:

Borrowing and paying back money is not always necessary to get credit. Most lenders are more than anxious to extend credit to consumers in order to collect inflated interest rates over an extended period of time.

But the Bible says to be aware because *"the borrower is slave to the lender"* (Proverbs 22:7).

Evelyn Adams can relate to Jimmy's lottery quandary. Incredibly, she wins the New Jersey lottery not just once, but two years in a row and takes home winnings totaling $5.4 million. Today she is broke and regrets she didn't utter the short, one-syllable two-letter word that would have helped preserve her savings—the word *no*. "Everybody wanted my money," she recalls. "Everybody had their hand out."[8]

But Evelyn readily admits she needed to be told *no* as well, describing herself as a big-time gambler continually drawn to the slot machines of Atlantic City. "I won the American Dream but I lost it, too. It was a very hard fall. It's called rock bottom."[9]

Evelyn and those who have gone from having riches to quickly losing them can identify with the words of Job:

> "He lies down wealthy, but will do so no more; when he opens his eyes, all is gone."
> (Job 27:19)

If you identify with Evelyn's financial discontent but not her draw to slot machines, you still may find that you are gambling with your financial security in other ways. A quick look at the following four tests will help you assess your own personal level of discontent and how it drives your money mismanagement.

#1 Do you pine after money—habitually longing for more?

The Hebrew word *keseph*, translated most often as "money," actually means "silver" (from its pale color). It is derived from the root word *kasaph*, which means "to become pale," by implication "to pine after."[10]

"Whoever loves money never has enough; whoever loves wealth is never satisfied with their income" (Ecclesiastes 5:10).

#2 Do you prioritize money over God?

In the New Testament the Aramaic word *mamonas*, translated "mammon" or "money," means "wealth." The word is defined as "material wealth or possessions especially as having a debasing influence."[11] This word is used to convey the concept that "money is deified" (worshiped as God).[12]

"No one can serve two masters. Either you will hate the one and love the other, or you will be devoted to the one and despise the other. You cannot serve both God and money" (Matthew 6:24).

#3 Can you be trusted to manage God's money wisely?

A Greek word translated as "manager" in the New Testament is *oikonomos*, which means "a manager or overseer."[13] It is also translated "one who has been given a trust" or "a trustee."

"Now it is required that those who have been given a trust must prove faithful" (1 Corinthians 4:2).

#4 Are you in financial bondage to credit lenders?

The Greek word *chreopheiletes* literally means "a debt-ower."[14] Found in the parable of the dishonest manager (Luke 16:1–13), this word points to the ancient system of extending credit.

"Let no debt remain outstanding, except the continuing debt to love one another, for whoever loves others has fulfilled the law" (Romans 13:8).

Prioritizing Money

QUESTION: "I'm truly grieving. I prioritized money over everything else. Now my wife has left me. What can I do?"

ANSWER: When you know you've been in the habit of "majoring on the minors," evaluate your choices. Typically, we learn *painful* lessons well! Plan now to change your priorities. Replace your bad decisions with these good decisions:

▶ Evaluate what you did wrong.

▶ Ask God to search your heart and reveal to you the lie you believed about money that led to your wrong thinking and behavior with respect to money.

▶ Genuinely repent by changing your mind about money and your actions regarding money.

▶ Make eternal investments by prioritizing people and relationships over financial gain.

▶ Admit to your wife that you were wrong and ask for her forgiveness.

▶ Explain to her what you are now doing differently.

Do not pressure her. She will see for herself if you have really changed from having an immature focus on money to having true maturity.

"The greedy bring ruin to their households ... " (Proverbs 15:27).

"Better a little with the fear of the LORD than great wealth with turmoil" (Proverbs 15:16).

Financial Boundaries

QUESTION: "How will having boundaries in the areas of my finances help me?"

ANSWER: Financial boundaries organize you to:

▶ Responsibly manage your budget and accounting procedures.

▶ Responsibly manage your spending and savings.

▶ Responsibly pay bills and meet other financial obligations on time.

▶ Responsibly make investments for the future.

▶ Responsibly make wills or trusts that place restrictions on how others use your resources.

▶ Responsibly make donations to the work of the Lord.

God shows us how to keep a balanced view of our monetary resources.

"Godliness with contentment is great gain. For we brought nothing into the world, and we can take nothing out of it. But if we have food and clothing, we will be content with that. Those who want to get rich fall into temptation and a trap and into many foolish and harmful desires that plunge people into ruin and destruction. For the love of money is a root of all kinds of evil. Some people, eager for money, have wandered from the faith and pierced themselves with many griefs" (1 Timothy 6:6–10).

WHAT IS God's Heart on Money?

William "Bud" Post, who won $16.2 million, wishes he had never won the lottery at all. Now content to live a quiet lifestyle with minimal income, Bud was traumatized by numerous lawsuits and hounded by siblings to invest in businesses that ultimately failed.

But Bud's most bitter betrayal came from a brother who hired a hit man to kill him in hopes of acquiring a portion of his winnings. It's safe to say that Bud will probably never buy another lottery ticket again, as he reflects. "I'm tired, I'm over 65 years old, and I just had a serious operation for a heart aneurysm. Lotteries don't mean (anything) to me."[15]

Winning the lottery presents a false promise of financial freedom, but the ultimate payout is often indescribable pain. Jesus warns us about what can harm our spiritual life.

> "Watch out! Be on your guard against all kinds of greed; life does not consist in an abundance of possessions."
> (Luke 12:15)

▶ **THE WORLD'S MIND-SET FOR MONEY:** To get what you want

GOD'S MIND-SET FOR MONEY: To give you what you need

"Do not worry, saying, 'What shall we eat?' or 'What shall we drink?' or 'What shall we wear?' For the pagans run after all these things, and your heavenly Father knows that you need them. But seek first his kingdom and his righteousness, and all these things will be given to you as well" (Matthew 6:31–33).

▶ **THE WORLD'S MIND-SET FOR MONEY:** To be used in whatever way you wish

GOD'S MIND-SET FOR MONEY: To be used only in trustworthy ways

"Whoever can be trusted with very little can also be trusted with much, and whoever is dishonest with very little will also be dishonest with much. So if you have not been trustworthy in handling worldly wealth, who will trust you with true riches?" (Luke 16:10–11).

▶ **THE WORLD'S MIND-SET FOR MONEY:** To gain temporary treasures

GOD'S MIND-SET FOR MONEY: To gather eternal treasures

"Do not store up for yourselves treasures on earth, where moths and vermin destroy, and where thieves break in and steal. But store up for yourselves treasures in heaven, where moths and vermin do not destroy, and where thieves do not break in and steal" (Matthew 6:19–20).

▶ **THE WORLD'S MIND-SET FOR MONEY:** To be valued above the soul

GOD'S MIND-SET FOR MONEY: To be used to bless the soul

"What good is it for someone to gain the whole world, yet forfeit their soul? Or what can anyone give in exchange for their soul?" (Mark 8:36–37).

▶ **THE WORLD'S MIND-SET FOR MONEY:** To trust in the power of possessions

GOD'S MIND-SET FOR MONEY: To trust in the power of God

"Some trust in chariots and some in horses, but we trust in the name of the LORD our God" (Psalm 20:7).

▶ **THE WORLD'S MIND-SET FOR MONEY:** To obtain personal power through possessions

GOD'S MIND-SET FOR MONEY: To demonstrate the Lord's power to provide

"'Bring the whole tithe into the storehouse, that there may be food in my house. Test me in this,' says the Lord Almighty, 'and see if I will not throw open the floodgates of heaven and pour out so much blessing that there will not be room enough to store it'" (Malachi 3:10).

▶ **THE WORLD'S MIND-SET FOR MONEY:** To selfishly build a personal kingdom

GOD'S MIND-SET FOR MONEY: To sacrificially share in God's kingdom

" ... they gave as much as they were able, and even beyond their ability. Entirely on their own, they urgently pleaded with us for the privilege of sharing in this service to the Lord's people. And they exceeded our expectations: They gave themselves first of all to the Lord and then by the will of God also to us" (2 Corinthians 8:3–5).

▶ **THE WORLD'S MIND-SET FOR MONEY:** To supply all of your needs apart from God

GOD'S MIND-SET FOR MONEY: To look to God to supply all of your needs

"And my God will meet all your needs according to the riches of his glory in Christ Jesus" (Philippians 4:19).

CHARACTERISTICS

"Come, see what our Father in heaven will do for us today," says George Müller.[16] The children stand and wait expectantly behind rows of chairs, anticipating word that breakfast is about to begin and they can take their seats. Their eyes gaze upon well-worn bowls and cups that line the long dining room table, but this particular morning there's something very different about the place settings before them. There is not a morsel of food in sight, nor even a sip of juice.

The orphans at Ashley Downs in England are accustomed to a nutritious meal to start their day, but now not only is there no food on the table, neither is there any food in the kitchen. The coffers to purchase oatmeal, bread, and fruit— are completely empty. Stomachs are rumbling as the breakfast hour quickly approaches. This only prompts the founder of the orphanage to do something most would consider unusual— *give thanks*.

The Bible encourages ....

"Rejoice always, pray continually,
give thanks in all circumstances;
for this is God's will for you in Christ Jesus."
(1 Thessalonians 5:16–18)

"Children," George Müller addresses, "it will soon be time for school, so let's pray. Dear Father, we thank you for what you are going to give us to eat."[17]

Suddenly there is a knock at the door. A local baker arrives with a special delivery. He explains, "I couldn't sleep last night. Somehow I felt you didn't have bread for breakfast, and the Lord wanted me to send you some. So I got up at two o'clock and baked some fresh bread for you."[18]

Müller praises God before the orphans and thanks the baker. Then a second knock is heard at the door. It is the community milkman, who tells Müller that his cart has broken down right by the orphanage and in order to fix it he must remove all of its contents. "Could the children use my cans of fresh milk?" he inquires.[19]

Müller experienced exceptional freedom, not from financial stress but from worry, debt, and anxiety due to his remarkable faith and dependence on God's provision. What a precious and timely gift!

> "That each of them may eat and drink,
> and find satisfaction in all their toil—
> this is the gift of God."
> (Ecclesiastes 3:13)

As you seek to determine the degree of your own financial freedom, it might prove helpful to look at the habits you have developed regarding the way you handle money.

Consider:

▶ Do you get cash advances from credit cards to pay other expenses?

▶ Do you pay only the minimum on credit card balances?

▶ Do you bounce checks or overdraw your bank account?

▶ Do you ignore the importance of having a savings account steadily accruing money?

▶ Do you use savings to pay credit card bills?

▶ Do you send in payments past the due dates?

▶ Do you avoid opening your mail?

▶ Do you wait until the last minute to pay your taxes?

▶ Do you have family conflicts over money?

If you answered *yes* to any of the preceding questions, you will need to make some adjustments to increase your level of financial freedom.

> "Let no debt remain outstanding,
> except the continuing debt to love
> one another, for whoever loves others
> has fulfilled the law."
> (Romans 13:8)

QUESTION: "My wife is pressuring me about spending more time with the family. How can I do that when she has a job and I am working two jobs in order to pay for our new house?"

ANSWER: When free time is rare, limits must necessarily be placed on how it is spent. One helpful activity would be for you and your wife to ...

▶ Sit down together and write out on a daily/hourly calendar the way you currently spend your time.

▶ Identify and reserve any free time you have to be spent with the family.

▶ Schedule your family time accordingly and determine to stick to your plan.

▶ Anticipate possible obstacles and set boundaries in place to guard and protect your schedule.

If you find there is no free time available, the two of you may need to ...

▶ Reevaluate your priorities regarding your time and where it will be best spent in relation to family and work.

▶ Determine whether you need to choose between having your new home or having more time with your family in a less expensive home.

Your priority needs to be placed on what is most important from God's eternal perspective rather than on what you may want and desire from a temporal, human perspective. Then you will spend your time supporting your value system, not undermining it, and you will reap eternal rewards.

Jesus said, *"Do not store up for yourselves treasures on earth, where moths and vermin destroy, and where thieves break in and steal. But store up for yourselves treasures in heaven, where moths and vermin do not destroy, and where thieves do not break in and steal"* (Matthew 6:19–20).

WHAT LIFESTYLES Lead to Debt?

Miracles sent from above—both material and monetary—were everyday occurrences in the life of George Müller, who died in March 1898 at the age of 92. The stalwart man of God found true financial freedom through faith, and he carefully guarded that precious privilege. Müller unashamedly depended daily on God for his physical and spiritual supplies, and that's why he found a gracious check that unexpectedly arrived in the mail unsettling.

A donation totaling almost $200 accompanies a letter indicating more financial help is on the way. The donor writes, "I think it right that some money should be provided for you. Though this is just a beginning, I hope many good Christians will add to it to form a fund to support you and your family."[20]

But what the donor perceives as right, Müller perceives as wrong according to the way he believes God wants to operate in his life. For Müller, the generous check and the promise of others serve not as a triumph but as a temptation to place his trust in a bank account instead of in his benevolent God. He doesn't want to put a stranglehold on his financial freedom by starting to worry about fluctuating figures in a balance column.

So Müller graciously returns the check, explaining that for most of his life he's never had a steady source of income nor has he ever lacked for anything.[21] When it comes to fiscal management, God can lead in many different ways, including receiving a salary and setting financial goals, but He leads everyone to rely on His provision and care.

The Bible instructs...

> "Command those who are rich in this present world not to be arrogant nor to put their hope in wealth, which is so uncertain, but to put their hope in God, who richly provides us with everything for our enjoyment."
> (1 Timothy 6:17)

Sometimes debt rises suddenly due to unexpected tragedy or illness. However, most of the time debt accrues gradually over time as a result of making numerous decisions based on a faulty belief system regarding money and God's purpose for it in our lives. A lifestyle then develops that leads to burgeoning debt that often leads in turn to bankruptcy and financial bondage. God never intends for His spiritual offspring to live in bondage, but rather in freedom.

> "I will walk about in freedom, for I have sought out your precepts."
> (Psalm 119:45)

Lifestyles That Lead to Debt

▶ **Living a Life of Faulty Values**

- Using money to keep up social appearances
- Using money to feel important
- Using money to manipulate others
- Using money to appear "righteous" in the eyes of God and others

    "Be careful not to practice your righteousness in front of others to be seen by them. If you do, you will have no reward from your Father in heaven" (Matthew 6:1).

▶ **Living a Life of Escape Mechanisms**

- Spending money to escape personal tensions
- Spending money to momentarily lift depression
- Spending money to indulge an obsession with a possession
- Spending money to buy love and affection

    "Those who work their land will have abundant food, but those who chase fantasies have no sense" (Proverbs 12:11).

    "The wise store up choice food, but fools gulp theirs down" (Proverbs 21:20).

▶ **Living a Life of Indolence**

- Seeking gain without working for it
- Seeking excuses for not having gainful employment

- Seeking wealth through "get-rich-quick" schemes
- Seeking self-employment to avoid accountability

"Lazy hands make for poverty, but diligent hands bring wealth" (Proverbs 10:4).

▶ LIVING A LIFE OF CREDIT AND BORROWING

- Borrowing to purchase depreciating items (things that decrease in value)
- Borrowing through means of credit cards (using the bank's money)
- Borrowing to invest in that over which you have no control (stock market)
- Borrowing large sums with compound interest (presuming on the future)

"Now listen, you who say, 'Today or tomorrow we will go to this or that city, spend a year there, carry on business and make money.' Why, you do not even know what will happen tomorrow. What is your life? You are a mist that appears for a little while and then vanishes" (James 4:13–14).

▶ LIVING A LIFE OF UNPREPAREDNESS

- Failing to take financial responsibility
- Failing to establish and follow a budget
- Failing to plan for the future
- Failing to live on one salary, when deemed necessary

"Give careful thought to your ways. You have planted much, but harvested little. You eat, but never have enough. You drink, but never have your fill. You put on clothes, but are not warm. You earn wages, only to put them in a purse with holes in it" (Haggai 1:5–6).

▶ LIVING A LIFE OF SELFISHNESS

- Neglecting to tithe
- Neglecting to pay debts
- Neglecting to save for the future
- Neglecting to help meet the needs of others

"Whoever sows sparingly will also reap sparingly, and whoever sows generously will also reap generously" (2 Corinthians 9:6).

WHAT CHARACTERIZES the Cords of Financial Bondage?

Trusting God moved Müller to not share his personal and ministry needs with others, but to lay them solely at the foot of the throne. God continually blessed and abundantly provided, including millions of dollars that blessed more than 10,000 orphans under his care. Müller has been aptly described as a man who "devised large and liberal things for the Lord's cause."[22]

Müller was led to share his needs with God alone, but God moves many other people to share their needs with others. Likewise, financial freedom can be found down various God-ordained paths. The key is to rely on God to provide by whatever means He chooses to enable the work He has planned.

> **"And God is able to bless you abundantly, so that in all things at all times, having all that you need, you will abound in every good work." (2 Corinthians 9:8)**

However, those who fail to trust God's provision can live in financial bondage. Following is an acrostic of the word BONDAGE that characterizes the lives of those trapped in disbelief.

Bitterness

When we are discontent with God or others over our finances, our anger spreads a deep root of underlying bitterness, affecting both us and those around us ...

▶ Focusing attention and energy on gaining possessions

▶ Indifference to the needs of others

▶ Resenting the position, prestige, power, and popularity of someone else

▶ Outbursts of anger that lead to sharp, cutting comments

▶ Nurturing an ungrateful attitude

▶ Being preoccupied by personal problems to the exclusion of concern for anyone else

"See to it that no one falls short of the grace of God and that no bitter root grows up to cause trouble and defile many" (Hebrews 12:15).

Overcommitment

Overcommitment to work leads to a life that is out of balance with what God desires. This workaholic lifestyle is centered around business to the exclusion of rest, relaxation, and relationships. Many Christians fall into this kind of bondage, which is also characterized by ...

▶ Rationalizing the need to overwork

▶ Carrying work everywhere

▶ Monopolizing every conversation with talk about work

▶ Lacking ability to truly enjoy time off or planned vacations because of work

▶ Feeling guilty when not working

▶ Keeping work projects generated in order to maintain a lifestyle of activity

"The blessing of the LORD brings wealth, without painful toil for it" (Proverbs 10:22).

Naiveté

To be naive is to be gullible and easily fooled by deception and dishonesty. To remain naive is to shun wise counsel and refuse to gain the knowledge needed to stop falling prey to dishonest deceivers. It is to continue ...

▶ Being easily tempted by "get-rich-quick" schemes

▶ Borrowing money to invest

▶ Lacking sales resistance

▶ Purchasing luxuries while neglecting needs

▶ Falling prey to frauds, swindlers, and unsound business ventures

▶ Making decisions out of emotional and spiritual immaturity

"The wisdom of the prudent is to give thought to their ways, but the folly of fools is deception" (Proverbs 14:8).

Dishonesty

Deceitfulness in finances is a subtle evil. It's usually the little, unseen deceptions that reveal a heart of insincerity, hypocrisy, lying, cheating, fraud, and stealing. It involves ...

▶ Thinking: "He will never know he gave me too much change."

▶ Believing: "Even though I have worn this, the store will take it back."

▶ Lying: "I'll just tell him the mower was broken when I borrowed it."

▶ Rationalizing: "I'll put this dinner with my family on the company expense account since we have to go out to eat because I had to work late."

▶ Theorizing: "I'll figure out how to make this expense tax deductible."

▶ Conniving: "I'll get my associate to find a way to legitimize this expenditure for me."

"If you have not been trustworthy with someone else's property, who will give you property of your own?" (Luke 16:12).

Anxiety

Anxiety involves uneasy feelings, apprehension, fear, worry, or emotional tension over ...

▶ Neglecting unpaid bills

▶ Overextending investments

▶ Incurring credit card debt

▶ Failing to have and regularly invest in a savings account

▶ Nurturing an obsessive ambition

▶ Lacking trust in God's provision

"Anxiety weighs down the heart ..." (Proverbs 12:25).

Greed

Greed is an insatiable thirst for *more*. To harbor greed is to reject God's right to rule and reign in your life and be the resource from which your every need is supplied. God is to be your Provider, the One you seek out to meet your needs, not material wealth, not ...

▶ Amassing power, prestige, or popularity to make sure you can get whatever you want from people

▶ Accruing money and wealth in order to buy whatever material possession your heart desires

▶ Accumulating precious stones, properties, or businesses so you will feel significant

▶ Storing up money in stocks or savings to insure financial security for the future

▶ Seeking to gain as much wealth as possible to become the envy of family members or friends

▶ Striving to acquire enough wealth to entice others to befriend you through giving them gifts

"Then he said to them, 'Watch out! Be on your guard against all kinds of greed; life does not consist in an abundance of possessions'" (Luke 12:15).

Envy

Envy is a resentful desire to have that which belongs to another. Envy grabs hold of a discontented heart by promising an increasing sense of worth but only causes pain ...

▶ Spreading corruption from the inside out

▶ Displaying constant discontent with people and life situations

▶ Developing into schemes for achieving success or acquiring possessions

▶ Encouraging self-interest and neglect of the needs of others

▶ Driving you to attack others in order to build yourself up

▶ Short-circuiting faith by demanding self-effort

"A heart at peace gives life to the body, but envy rots the bones" (Proverbs 14:30).

Possessed by Possessions— The Rich Fool

Luke 12:13–21

A man came out of the crowd that was following Jesus and asked Him to tell his brother to relinquish his share of their inheritance. (According to Jewish law, the eldest brother would be responsible for maintaining the family resources.) Jesus did not get drawn into family property disputes, but He did speak to the heart of the matter by warning the crowd about greed.

Jesus then told a story about a rich man who had accumulated an overabundance of things. Then the man said, "I'll build bigger barns to store all this wealth." While the rich fool was content in his false security, Jesus warned, *"This very night your life will be demanded from you. Then who will get what you have prepared for yourself?"* (Luke 12:20). Jesus warns against having a love of material security instead of a heart that invests in the things of God.

"For of this you can be sure:
No immoral, impure or greedy person—
such a person is an idolater—
has any inheritance in the kingdom
of Christ and of God."
(Ephesians 5:5)

CAUSES OF FINANCIAL BONDAGE

The biblical word *mammon* is unfamiliar to most people today. The term now used more frequently in reference to a preoccupation with wealth and riches is *materialism*.

But whether you call it materialism or mammon worship, it has nothing to do with how much or how little you have, but everything to do with your heart! Both the rich and the poor can be materialistic, but the heart can worship and serve only one God!

> "No one can serve two masters.
> Either you will hate the one
> and love the other,
> or you will be devoted to the one
> and despise the other.
> You cannot serve both God and money."
> (Matthew 6:24)

The giants of the gridiron are modern-day gladiators who earn multiple millions of dollars running up points on a scoreboard and elating football fans across the U.S. The players of the National Football League hold considerable prestige. Their athletic prowess carries them to the top of their game, and their lavish lifestyles indulge the imaginations of both young and old alike.

But, alas, even giants can fall. A debilitating physical injury can permanently sideline a professional football player. Statistics point to yet another common vulnerability—financial mismanagement. Within two years of retirement from the NFL, 78% of players either have declared bankruptcy or are experiencing severe financial stress due to divorce or joblessness. The statistics show that players in the National Basketball Association don't fare much better.[23]

It is easy to be critical of professional athletes, but what about your attitude toward wealth? Do you sit in church on Sunday morn, giving evidence to your Christian claim, but all the while your heart's divided, only obsessed with earthly gain?

If your answer to the above question is *yes*, listen to the words of Jesus:

> **"If a house is divided against itself,**
> **that house cannot stand."**
> **(Mark 3:25)**

The Heart That Harbors Materialism

▶ Do I have a heart that is proud?

"Humility is the fear of the LORD; its wages are riches and honor and life" (Proverbs 22:4).

▶ Do I have a heart that is selfish?

"Turn my heart toward your statutes and not toward selfish gain" (Psalm 119:36).

▶ Do I have a heart that is impatient?

"The prudent see danger and take refuge, but the simple keep going and pay the penalty" (Proverbs 22:3).

▶ Do I have a heart that seeks to serve others more than serving God?

"Whatever you do, work at it with all your heart, as working for the Lord, not for human masters, since you know that you will receive an inheritance from the Lord as a reward. It is the Lord Christ you are serving" (Colossians 3:23–24).

▶ Do I have a heart that is lazy?

"A little sleep, a little slumber, a little folding of the hands to rest—and poverty will come on you like a thief and scarcity like an armed man" (Proverbs 6:10–11).

▶ Do I have a heart that is stingy?

"The stingy are eager to get rich and are unaware that poverty awaits them" (Proverbs 28:22).

▶ Do I have a heart that lacks faith?

"Let us draw near to God with a sincere heart and with the full assurance that faith brings ... " (Hebrews 10:22).

▶ Do I have a heart that lacks wisdom, understanding, and knowledge?

"By wisdom a house is built, and through understanding it is established; through knowledge its rooms are filled with rare and beautiful treasures" (Proverbs 24:3–4).

▶ Do I have a heart that is unthankful?

"Do not be anxious about anything, but in every situation, by prayer and petition, with thanksgiving, present your requests to God" (Philippians 4:6).

▶ Do I have a heart that lacks joy in giving?

"Each of you should give what you have decided in your heart to give, not reluctantly or under compulsion, for God loves a cheerful giver" (2 Corinthians 9:7).

Parables, Money, and Greed

QUESTION: "Many parables that Jesus told focus on handling money. Why did Jesus link our spiritual condition so closely with finances?"

ANSWER: Many of Jesus' parables deal with the relationship between money and our spiritual motivation. Perhaps the reason is that the two basic sins of *idolatry* and *greed* are closely associated with the love of money. If we refuse to allow God to be Lord in our hearts and Lord of our lives and refuse to depend on Him to meet all of our needs, we don't have many options to choose from other than false gods. And money is definitely a false god to many.

"Among you there must not be even a hint of sexual immorality, or of any kind of impurity, or of greed, because these are improper for God's holy people" (Ephesians 5:3).

A myriad of reasons reveal how athletes nosedive financially. This is the focus of a popular documentary series on ESPN titled "Broke." One compelling reason is the pressure to impress peers, both on and off the playing field. If a teammate shows up in the locker room sporting a $20,000 diamond-studded watch, someone else will be wearing a $25,000 watch the next day.

Andre Rison, who was a wide receiver for several pro football teams, states unequivocally: "I guarantee you, I spent a million dollars on jewelry."[24]

Such displays of trophies and treasures are similar to the *"spoils of war"* captured in battle. *"Their camels will become plunder, and their large herds will be spoils of war"* (Jeremiah 49:32).

The Bible reveals stories of many who measured their worth by the wealth or possessions they acquired. Materialistic attitudes brought unexpected outcomes, showing that the pursuit of temporary material riches results in the loss of true eternal treasure.

There is no substitute for God, and there is no provision for those who choose the temporal over the eternal. God created us for Himself and made us to be dependent on nothing but Himself. The following true situations demonstrate this fact.

▶ **The Soldier of Fortune (Joshua 7)**

Achan was a soldier in Joshua's army who had taken part in the great defeat of Jericho. He knew of God's conditions for victory. He knew that the valuable spoils of war were sacred and must go into God's treasury. Otherwise, Israel would experience destruction. Yet Achan had disobeyed the Lord. His desire for material fortune overcame his will to obey God. He had taken silver, gold, and money, along with a beautiful Babylonian garment. When Joshua cried out to God at his subsequent defeat by the Amorites, the Lord told him that it was because there was sin in the camp. Achan was exposed and experienced the judgment of God. He and his family were stoned to death and burned along with all their possessions.

"Whoever is caught with the devoted things shall be destroyed by fire, along with all that belongs to him. He has violated the covenant of the Lord and has done an outrageous thing in Israel!" (Joshua 7:15).

▶ **The Conspiring Church Couple (Acts 4:32–5:10)**

Ananias and Sapphira, a couple in the early church at Jerusalem, sold some property and presented some of the proceeds from the sale to the apostles. At that time, the attitude of the believers in the church was that everything each member possessed was held in common by all the members. As needs would arise, one of the members who held property would sell it and give all the income to the apostles to meet the presenting need. The problem with Annanias and Sapphira was that they sought to deceive the apostles, the church, and God by claiming they gave all the money from the sale, while in reality they held back some of it for themselves. Bottom line, they lied to God, and their deception was discovered through a revelation of the Holy Spirit, resulting in the death of both deceivers.

"Peter said to her, 'How could you conspire to test the Spirit of the Lord? Listen! The feet of the men who buried your husband are at the door, and they will carry you out also.' At that moment she fell down at his feet and died" (Acts 5:9–10).

WHAT IS the Root Cause of Financial Bondage?

Besides competitive behavior, greed can get the best of athletes until a compilation of cars, yachts, and other expensive "toys" siphons away savings. Leon Searcy, a former offensive lineman, received an injury settlement of $60,000 after being released from his team. His ex-wife got $6,000 for child support and Leon's remaining share of $54,000 never even made it into a savings account. He paid $50,000 in cash for a luxury vehicle because "I had to have it."[25]

Jesus gives this warning in Scripture: *"Watch out! Be on your guard against all kinds of greed; life does not consist in an abundance of possessions"* (Luke 12:15).

Materialism is more than just a desire for material gain. Since God has given you three inner needs—the needs for love, significance, and security[26]—when you seek to meet these needs through any means other than trusting in God, those substitutes take the place of God in your life. This can be called "idolatry."

Materialism is placing trust in worldly wealth to meet your inner needs for love, significance, and security. When wealth is not achieved or fails to satisfy, an underlying sense of discontentment is felt, no matter your circumstances.

Men tend to see their identity as being in work and worldly ambitions. This mind-set often leads them to have the false belief that financial success and accumulation of wealth will fill their need for *significance*—a sense of importance to their families and position among their peers. The need for *security* is usually stronger in women, causing many to place their hope in the false security of material wealth. When married, women often seek their own value and worth in the financial success of their husbands.

Both men and women can forfeit financial freedom in their quest for *love*. While the familiar adage, "Money can't buy love or happiness," is often quoted, those hungry for love and approval spend beyond their means in an attempt to lure someone into an intimate loving relationship with them.

Three God-Given Inner Needs

In reality, we have all been created with three God-given inner needs: the needs for love, significance, and security.

▶ **Love**—to know that someone is unconditionally committed to our best interest

"My command is this: Love each other as I have loved you" (John 15:12).

▶ **Significance**—to know that our lives have meaning and purpose

"I cry out to God Most High, to God who fulfills his purpose for me" (Psalm 57:2 ESV).

▶ **Security**—to feel accepted and a sense of belonging

"Whoever fears the LORD has a secure fortress, and for their children it will be a refuge" (Proverbs 14:26).

The Ultimate Need-Meeter

Why did God give us these deep inner needs, knowing that people fail people and self-effort fails us as well?

God gave us these inner needs so that we would come to know Him as our Need-Meeter. Our needs are designed by God to draw us into a deeper dependence on Christ. God did not create any person or position or any amount of power or possessions to meet the deepest needs in our lives. If a person or thing could meet all our needs, we wouldn't need God! The Lord will use circumstances and bring positive people into our lives as an extension of His care and compassion, but ultimately only God can satisfy all the needs of our hearts. The Bible says ...

> "The LORD will guide you always; he will satisfy your needs in a sun-scorched land and will strengthen your frame.
> You will be like a well-watered garden, like a spring whose waters never fail."
> (Isaiah 58:11)

The apostle Paul revealed this truth by first asking, *"What a wretched man I am. Who will rescue me from this body that is subject to death?"* and then by answering his own question in saying it is *"Jesus Christ our Lord!"* (Romans 7:24–25).

All along, the Lord planned to meet our deepest needs for ...

▶ **Love**—*"I* [the Lord] *have loved you with an everlasting love; I have drawn you with unfailing kindness"* (Jeremiah 31:3).

▶ **Significance**—*"'For I know the plans I have for you,' declares the LORD, 'plans to prosper you and not to harm you, plans to give you hope and a future'"* (Jeremiah 29:11).

▶ **Security**—*"The LORD himself goes before you and will be with you; he will never leave you nor forsake you. Do not be afraid; do not be discouraged"* (Deuteronomy 31:8).

The truth is that our God-given needs for love, significance, and security can be legitimately met in Christ Jesus! Philippians 4:19 makes it plain ...

> **"My God will meet all your needs according to the riches of his glory in Christ Jesus."**

▶ **Wrong Beliefs:**

For Love: "I'll be content when I have enough money to attract anyone I desire—then I'll really feel loved."

For Significance: "I'll be content when I have enough money to impress others and achieve power—then I'll feel significant."

For Security: "I'll be content when I have enough money to meet all my needs—then I'll feel secure about the future."

▶ **Right Belief:**

"Contentment is not found in how much I have or in any amount of wealth. Contentment comes through trusting God to meet all my needs and by being conformed to the character of Christ."

" ... I have learned to be content whatever the circumstances. I know what it is to be in need, and I know what it is to have plenty. I have learned the secret of being content in any and every situation, whether well fed or hungry, whether living in plenty or in want. ... And my God will meet all your needs according to the riches of his glory in Christ Jesus" (Philippians 4:11–12, 19).

One of the most significant questions in Scripture comes from the rich young man who asked Jesus, *"Teacher, what good thing must I do to get eternal life?"* Jesus replied, *"If you want to enter life, keep the commandments."* This young man was obviously a man of good character, for he had kept the commandments that Jesus named, yet the man knew something was missing. After evaluating his behavior, the man asked, *"What do I still lack?"* (Matthew 19:16–17, 20). Jesus' answer went straight to the core of the man's heart, bringing to light what he treasured most.

"'If you want to be perfect, go, sell your possessions and give to the poor, and you will have treasure in heaven. Then come, follow me.' When the young man heard this, he went away sad, because he had great wealth" (Matthew 19:21–22).

The tragedy wasn't that the young man possessed wealth but that his wealth possessed him. He couldn't follow Jesus' command because money held the highest place in his heart. He didn't understand that true treasure begins not with *material* wealth, but with *spiritual* wealth, and the greatest treasure is a relationship with God's Son, Jesus. With Him you can have not only eternal life, but you can also have peace and security regardless of your financial situation. And if you submit your income and spending to Him, you'll have God's wisdom to help you live in financial freedom.

How to Have the Treasure of a Relationship with Jesus

Four Points of God's Plan

#1 God's Purpose for You is *Salvation*.

What was God's motivation in sending Jesus Christ to earth?

To express His love for you by saving you! The Bible says ...

"God so loved the world that he gave his one and only Son, that whoever believes in him shall not perish but have eternal life. For God did not send his Son into the world to condemn the world, but to save the world through him" (John 3:16–17).

What was Jesus' purpose in coming to earth?

To forgive your sins, to empower you to have victory over sin, and to enable you to live a fulfilled life! Jesus said ...

"I have come that they may have life, and that they may have it more abundantly" (John 10:10 NKJV).

#2 Your Problem is *Sin*.

What exactly is sin?

Sin is living independently of God's standard—knowing what is right, but choosing what is wrong. The Bible says ...

"If anyone, then, knows the good they ought to do and doesn't do it, it is sin for them" (James 4:17).

Spiritual death, eternal separation from God. Scripture states ...

"Your iniquities [sins] have separated you from your God" (Isaiah 59:2).

"The wages of sin is death, but the gift of God is eternal life in Christ Jesus our Lord" (Romans 6:23).

#3 God's Provision for You is the *Savior.*

Yes! Jesus died on the cross to personally pay the penalty for your sins. The Bible says ...

"God demonstrates his own love for us in this: While we were still sinners, Christ died for us" (Romans 5:8).

Belief in (entrusting your life to) Jesus Christ as the only way to God the Father. Jesus says ...

"I am the way and the truth and the life. No one comes to the Father except through me" (John 14:6).

"Believe in the Lord Jesus, and you will be saved" (Acts 16:31).

#4 Your Part is *Surrender.*

Give Christ control of your life, entrusting yourself to Him.

"Jesus said to his disciples, 'Whoever wants to be my disciple must deny themselves and take up their cross [die to your own self-rule] *and follow me. For whoever wants to save their life will lose it, but whoever loses their life for me will find it. What good will it be for someone to gain the whole world, yet forfeit their soul?'"* (Matthew 16:24–26).

Place your faith in (rely on) Jesus Christ as your personal Lord and Savior and reject your "good works" as a means of earning God's approval.

"It is by grace you have been saved, through faith—and this is not from yourselves, it is the gift of God —not by works, so that no one can boast." (Ephesians 2:8–9)

The moment you choose to receive Jesus as your Lord and Savior—entrusting your life to Him—His Spirit comes to live inside you. Then He empowers you to live the fulfilled life God has planned for you.

If you want to be fully forgiven by God and become the person God created you to be, you can tell Him in a simple, heartfelt prayer like this:

PRAYER OF SALVATION

"God, I want a real relationship with You.
I admit that many times I've chosen
to go my own way instead of Your way.
Please forgive me for my sins.
Jesus, thank You for dying on the cross
to pay the penalty for my sins.
Come into my life to be
my Lord and my Savior.
Holy Spirit, Change me from the
inside out and make me the person
You created me to be.
In Your holy name I pray. Amen."

What Can You Now Expect?

If you sincerely prayed this prayer, look at what God says about you!

"Truly I tell you, whoever hears my word
and believes him who sent me
has eternal life and will not be judged
but has crossed over from death to life."
(John 5:24)

STEPS TO SOLUTION

The first chapter of the book of Haggai contains the reason for and the solution to the financial woes experienced by the nation of Israel years ago and to much of our financial woes today as well. Israel dishonored God by not prioritizing Him or His house over themselves and were suffering the consequences of their self-centered choices. Not once, but *twice* the Lord spoke these words to them, words we all need to hear and heed to this very day, *"Give careful thought to your ways."*

"This is what the Lord Almighty says:
'Give careful thought to your ways.
You have planted much, but harvested little.
You eat, but never have enough.
You drink, but never have your fill.
You put on clothes, but are not warm.
You earn wages, only to put them in
a purse with holes in it.' ...
'Why?' declares the Lord Almighty.
'Because of my house, which remains a ruin,
while each of you is busy
with your own house.'"
(Haggai 1:5–6, 9)

Key Verses to Memorize

The following words in the Gospel of Luke are just as true today as when Jesus spoke them, and they will remain true as long as this world exists.

These words clearly identify the correlation between being trustworthy with worldly wealth and being trusted with eternal riches.

> *"Whoever can be trusted with very little can also be trusted with much, and whoever is dishonest with very little will also be dishonest with much. So if you have not been trustworthy in handling worldly wealth, who will trust you with true riches?"*
> (Luke 16:10–11)

Checklist for
Trustworthy Spending

How can you know whether you are trustworthy in the way you handle money? You must first desire to please the Lord in every way when it comes to managing the financial resources He entrusts to your care. Therefore, before you purchase anything, ask yourself:

☐ "Is this purchase a true *need* or a mere *desire*?"

☐ "Do I have adequate funds to purchase this without using credit?"

☐ "Have I compared the cost of competitive products?"

☐ "Have I prayed about this purchase?"

☐ "Have I been patient in waiting on God's provision?"

☐ "Do I have God's peace regarding this purchase?"

☐ "Does this purchase conform to the purpose God has for me?"

☐ "Does my spouse agree with me (if you are married) about this purchase?"

When it comes to pleasing the Lord, we all want to hear Him say, *"'Well done, my good servant!' his master replied, 'Because you have been trustworthy in a very small matter, take charge of ten cities'"* (Luke 19:17).

Key Passage to Read

Words Jesus spoke regarding the worthlessness of worry contain truths that can effectively set you free from financial bondage. In this passage from the Sermon on the Mount, Jesus spells out the relationship between you and your heavenly Father and how He will meet your needs.

MATTHEW 6:25–34

WHY WORRY?

▶ **Life consists of more than food, drink, or clothing** (v. 25).

So why do you worry?

▶ **God takes care of the birds. He will assuredly take care of you** (v. 26).

So why do you worry?

▶ **You can't add one moment to your life** (v. 27).

So why do you worry?

▶ **God dresses His fields with majestic flowers. He will clothe you with far greater glory** (v. 28).

So why do you worry?

▶ **Human wealth and wisdom can never provide anything comparable to God's provisions** (v. 29).

So why do you worry?

▶ **You are more valuable to God than all else He has created** (v. 30).

So why do you worry?

▶ **God doesn't want you to worry at all about the things you need** (v. 31).

So why do you worry?

▶ **Your heavenly Father knows just what you need** (v. 32).

So why do you worry?

▶ **Your goal is to obey God's Word, be Christlike in character, and He will meet your needs** (v. 33).

So why do you worry?

▶ **Refuse to be uneasy about the future. Live and trust God one day at a time** (v. 34).

So why do you worry?

Savings Accounts

QUESTION: **"I've been told it is wrong to save money. Does a savings account prove that I'm not trusting God?"**

ANSWER: God does want us to be responsible with our finances, and it's not wrong to save for future needs. There are many Scriptures that support having and maintaining storehouses, even in the temple of God. (See Genesis 6:20–22; 41:34–36; 2 Kings 20:13; Proverbs 6:6–8; 13:22; 21:20.) But when worry about financial security causes us to become money-focused rather than God-focused and to place our *hope* in material wealth or to *hoard* what we have for the future, we are guilty of distrusting God.

God calls a few to depend totally on Him to miraculously provide for all their needs. However, even the apostle Paul labored for his keep. Pray and ask God what His will is for you in this particular area. Jesus spoke to both scenarios—storing up earthly wealth while lacking spiritual riches and storing up treasures in heaven.

"But God said to him, 'You fool! This very night your life will be demanded from you. Then who will get what you have prepared for yourself?' This is how it will be with whoever stores up things for themselves but is not rich toward God" (Luke 12:20–21).

"Do not store up for yourselves
treasures on earth,
where moths and vermin destroy,
and where thieves break in and steal.
But store up for yourselves treasures
in heaven, where moths and vermin
do not destroy, and where thieves
do not break in and steal."
(Matthew 6:19–20)

God has given every Christian a new life, and with that new life comes three new targets: a new purpose, a new priority, and a new plan. If you desire to live a life that glorifies God and brings fulfillment to you, the first step is realizing that the Spirit of God lives within you as your Lord, making Him your master, ruler, and owner. Secondly, know that He has a perfect plan for your life—a plan He will guide you to, walk you through, and empower you to accomplish.

"I know the plans I have for you,' declares the LORD, 'plans to prosper you and not to harm you, plans to give you hope and a future'" (Jeremiah 29:11).

God will supply you with the desire and the strength to be the person He created you to be. Your part is to cooperate with Him by committing yourself to Him and setting your sights on ...

Reaching the Target

Target #1—A New Purpose: God's purpose for me is to be conformed to the character of Christ.

> *"Those God foreknew he also predestined to be conformed to the image of his Son ..."* (Romans 8:29).

- "I'll do whatever it takes to be conformed to the character of Christ."

Target #2—A New Priority: God's priority for me is to change my thinking.

"Do not conform to the pattern of this world, but be transformed by the renewing of your mind" (Romans 12:2).

- "I'll do whatever it takes to line up my thinking with God's thinking."

Target #3—A New Plan: God's plan for me is to rely on Christ's strength, not my strength, to be all He created me to be.

"I can do all things through him who strengthens me" (Philippians 4:13 ESV).

- "I'll do whatever it takes to fulfill His plan in His strength."

My Personalized Plan

As I set my sights on the three new targets God has set before me, my personalized plan will be to practice these five principles of managing money. In doing so, I will seek to find ...

▶ Freedom through Contentment

▶ Freedom through Self-Control

▶ Freedom through Stewardship

▶ Freedom through Giving

▶ Freedom through Petition

With each step I take in my personalized plan, I will commit myself and all that I do to the Lord.

> "Commit to the LORD whatever you do,
> and he will establish your plans."
> (Proverbs 16:3)

"The rich rule over the poor, and the borrower is slave to the lender" (Proverbs 22:7).

Dave Ramsey knows what it's like to be in bondage. Like the proverb describes, he was a borrowing slave to the lender and vows never again to drag around the ball and chain of debt.

"I knew hurt," he recalls while reflecting on a financial crisis he experienced as a young adult. After graduating from the University of Tennessee with a business degree, Dave wastes no time applying his knowledge and skills in real estate. By age 26 Dave accumulates $4 million in assets, set for stellar success until a devastating financial crash shatters the real estate market and banks call in his notes. Dave loses everything—including his home and almost his marriage. Before he can attempt to rebuild his personal finances, he is forced to file for bankruptcy. After this debilitating crisis, he learns wiser investment strategies and other valuable lessons.[27] Eventually Dave achieves lasting financial success and now shares money management principles that truly work.

The question you must answer is whether or not you are ready to change and begin to value and understand the wisdom of managing money.

"Why should fools have money in hand to buy wisdom, when they are not able to understand it?" (Proverbs 17:16).

Five Principles of Managing Money

Principle #1—Freedom through Contentment

As the saying goes, "Life is a series of choices," and contentment is one of those choices God wants you to make, especially with regard to money. When you look to money instead of to God to bring meaning to your life, the trouble it brings is terrible.

> "The fear of the Lord leads to life; then one rests content, untouched by trouble."
> (Proverbs 19:23)

▶ **Remind** yourself—God owns everything!

" ... *the world is mine, and all that is in it*" (Psalm 50:12).

▶ **Recognize** God as the source—He provides all you possess.

"You may say to yourself, 'My power and the strength of my hands have produced this wealth for me.' But remember the Lord your God, for it is he who gives you the ability to produce wealth" (Deuteronomy 8:17–18).

▶ **Realize** that God wants you to be content with what you have—He wants you to be like Him.

"Godliness with contentment is great gain. ... But if we have food and clothing, we will be content with that" (1 Timothy 6:6, 8).

▶ **Review** the ways God has provided for your needs in the past—He is always faithful.

*"So Abraham called that place The L*ORD* Will Provide. And to this day it is said, 'On the mountain of the L*ORD* it will be provided'"* (Genesis 22:14).

▶ **Rest** in the assurance of God's love regardless of your financial circumstances—He is always with you.

"Keep your lives free from the love of money and be content with what you have, because God has said, 'Never will I leave you; never will I forsake you'" (Hebrews 13:5).

▶ **Rely** on the faithfulness of God—He is trustworthy.

*"And he passed in front of Moses, proclaiming, 'The L*ORD*, the L*ORD*, the compassionate and gracious God, slow to anger, abounding in love and faithfulness'"* (Exodus 34:6).

QUESTION: "Why is money so important to me? Does it symbolize more than the obvious?"

ANSWER: Absolutely! Money can be made a substitute for just about anything because it is the means by which many purchase pleasurable experiences. Money buys much but it cannot buy what cannot be sold. It cannot buy the essential intangibles in life. It cannot meet the inner needs of the soul and spirit. As you seek to examine your view of money, ask God to show you what symbolism money might have for you.

Does money symbolize ...

- Security?
- Power?
- Significance?
- Independence?
- Self-worth?
- A means to help others?
- Status?
- Other?

Once you discover the needs you expect money to fill, quote this Scripture repeatedly and ask God to make it real in your heart whenever you are tempted to spend needlessly.

> **"My God will meet all your needs according to the riches of his glory in Christ Jesus."**
> **(Philippians 4:19)**

Principle #2—Freedom through Self-Control

Since you died with Christ to the power of sin in your life, you must choose to consider yourself dead to the strong pull of sin and act accordingly by exercising self-control.

> **"Put to death, therefore, whatever belongs to your earthly nature ... evil desires and greed, which is idolatry."**
> **(Colossians 3:5)**

▶ **Start** by mentally and emotionally transferring ownership of everything you own to God.

- Believe in God's sovereignty over you and all you possess.
- Believe in God's ability to know what is best for you.
- Believe in God's power to do what is best for you.

   "'The silver is mine and the gold is mine,' declares the LORD Almighty" (Haggai 2:8).

▶ **Separate** yourself from the financial sins of greed and idolatry.

- Repent and confess if your trust is in money.
- Realize that you may be enslaved by this sin.
- Remind yourself of the consequences of financial bondage.

   "Those who trust in their riches will fall ... " (Proverbs 11:28).

▶ **Set** a new goal for managing your finances.

- Make it your goal to counsel with someone who has financial self-control.
- Make it your goal to follow God's plan for your finances.
- Make it your goal to become wise with the money He entrusts to you.

   "Instruct the wise and they will be wiser still; teach the righteous and they will add to their learning" (Proverbs 9:9).

▶ **Stand** on truth when tempted to make unwise financial decisions.

- Know that in Christ you are free from the bondage of sin.
- Know that in Christ you are free from the power of sin.
- Know that in Christ you are "dead to sin."

  "We know that our old self was crucified with him so that the body ruled by sin might be done away with, that we should no longer be slaves to sin" (Romans 6:6).

▶ **Surrender** your will to the will of God.

- Acknowledge that you belong to God.
- Acknowledge that God has authority over everything you own.
- Acknowledge that the decision is yours. You have the *choice* to obey or to disobey God.

  "Just as you used to offer yourselves as slaves to impurity and to ever-increasing wickedness, so now offer yourselves as slaves to righteousness leading to holiness" (Romans 6:19).

▶ **Stay** away from temptation by controlling your thoughts.

- Avoid thinking that you alone are in control of your finances.
- Avoid thinking it is okay to occasionally indulge yourself.
- Avoid thinking that you can do whatever you want through your own self-sufficiency.

"No temptation has overtaken you except what is common to mankind. And God is faithful; he will not let you be tempted beyond what you can bear. But when you are tempted, he will also provide a way out so that you can endure it" (1 Corinthians 10:13).

QUESTION: "Will I be wealthy if I follow God's financial principles for managing money?"

ANSWER: God gives *no guarantees* that you will be monetarily wealthy, but obedience always brings spiritual rewards in this life as well as rewards in the life to come. Poverty plagues our world, and those blessed with wealth do not always acknowledge God as the owner of all.

However, God does give us many principles in the Bible to help us become wise in the matter of money so that it will be a blessing to us and not a curse. Ultimately, we are to trust in His sovereign control over all things, knowing that He does have a plan and a purpose.

As the Bible says ...

> "Rich and poor have this in common:
> The LORD is the Maker of them all."
> (Proverbs 22:2)

Principle #3—Freedom through Stewardship

Jesus told a parable explaining both the earthly and heavenly benefit of being a faithful steward, and He made this pronouncement we all long to hear one day.

> "Well done, good and faithful servant!
> You have been faithful with a few things;
> I will put you in charge of many things.
> Come and share your master's happiness!"
> (Matthew 25:23)

▶ **Recognize** your accountability to God for how you spend money.

- **Know** exactly what comes in.
- **Know** exactly what goes out.
- **Know** exactly where it goes (budgeting).
- **Know** how to save (regardless of your income).
- **Know** how to put your money to work for you (safe investment planning).
- **Know** how to plan for your future (retirement planning).

"What will I do when God confronts me? What will I answer when called to account?" (Job 31:14).

▶ **Return** the first tenth of your earnings to God—this must be a commitment.

- **Plan** your budget with the idea of including a set amount to give back to God on a weekly or monthly basis, depending on when you receive income.

- **Plan** the exact amount of your tithe according to your income before taxes or anything else is taken from it.

- **Plan** the amount of your tithe and any gift above that with your spouse (if you are married).

- **Plan** to pray both alone and with your spouse for an agreed on period of time before coming together and sharing what the Lord has laid on each of your hearts to give.

- **Plan** ahead of time the means by which you will give your gift to God—whether by check, automatic withdrawal, money order, cash, or some other method.

- **Plan** a time to pray and determine the recipients of your tithe and offerings to God's work and the amount each will receive.

"A tithe of everything from the land, whether grain from the soil or fruit from the trees, belongs to the Lord; it is holy to the Lord" (Leviticus 27:30).

▶ **Refuse** to live your life deluged, defeated, and deflated by debt.

- **Debt** puts you in bondage to another person, company, or institution.

- **Debt** may show a lack of trust in God to provide for your needs.

- **Debt** may reveal a lack of self-control, one of the fruits of the Spirit.

- **Debt** violates Scripture in that you are to be free of debt except the debt to love others.

- **Debt** produces worry, anxiety, and stress, all of which hinder your ability to serve God freely and focus on Him completely.

- **Debt** promises happiness but brings pain.

"There is a way that appears to be right, but in the end it leads to death" (Proverbs 14:12).

QUESTION: "What is a tithe?"

ANSWER: The word *tithe* literally means a "tenth." The act of tithing is giving an offering—a voluntary contribution of one tenth of your income—to God and, therefore, to the ministry of God on earth.

The first tithe mentioned in the Bible dates back 430 years *before the Law* was even given by God to Moses. After rescuing his nephew Lot from four enemy kings, Abram gave a tithe to show his deep gratitude to God. Abram gave—*"a tenth of everything"* (Genesis 14:20).

QUESTION: "The government is wasteful and often makes immoral decisions. Isn't it better to not pay taxes and give that money to more worthy causes?"

ANSWER: No. The Bible states that every government has the authority to collect taxes. Therefore, you should be faithful to pay what is due to the government. You can't obey God and at the same time disobey the tax law instituted by an authority established by God.

"Let everyone be subject to the governing authorities, for there is no authority except that which God has established. The authorities that exist have been established by God. ... This is also why you pay taxes, for the authorities are God's servants, who give their full time to governing" (Romans 13:1, 6).

Principle #4—Freedom through Giving

Your heavenly Father is the giver of all good gifts and in your desire to be like Him it stands to reason that you would imitate Him by cheerfully and generously giving good things to others.

"Every good and perfect gift is from above, coming down from the Father of the heavenly lights, who does not change like shifting shadows." (James 1:17)

▶ **Give confidently** to God that which He has commanded.

"Honor the LORD with your possessions, and with the firstfruits of all your increase" (Proverbs 3:9 NKJV).

▶ **Give regularly** to the work of the Lord.

"On the first day of every week, each one of you should set aside a sum of money in keeping with your income, saving it up, so that when I come no collections will have to be made" (1 Corinthians 16:2).

▶ **Give sacrificially** by giving up some of your own desires.

"I testify that they gave as much as they were able, and even beyond their ability" (2 Corinthians 8:3).

▶ **Give cheerfully**, not reluctantly or under pressure.

"Each of you should give what you have decided in your heart to give, not reluctantly or under compulsion, for God loves a cheerful giver" (2 Corinthians 9:7).

▶ **Give generously** to the poor and needy.

"Whoever oppresses the poor shows contempt for their Maker, but whoever is kind to the needy honors God" (Proverbs 14:31).

▶ **Give compassionately** in response to the needs of other Christians.

"Share with the Lord's people who are in need. Practice hospitality" (Romans 12:13).

▶ **Give secretly**, without letting others know.

"… do not let your left hand know what your right hand is doing, so that your giving may be in secret. Then your Father, who sees what is done in secret, will reward you" (Matthew 6:3–4).

QUESTION: "How important is the amount of my gift?"

ANSWER: The issue is not how big your gift is, but how big your faith is. Perhaps the most famous gift of all came from the poorest person of all. (Read Mark 12:41–44.) *"They all gave out of their wealth; but she, out of her poverty, put in everything—all she had to live on"* (Mark 12:44).

PRINCIPLE #5—FREEDOM THROUGH PETITION— HOW TO PRAY FOR YOUR NEEDS

While your heavenly Father knows your needs even before you do and has already set in motion His plan for meeting them, He still wants the interaction with you that occurs when you share those needs with Him and ask Him to meet them in His way and in His time. What parent wouldn't want that from their child?

> "And pray in the Spirit on all occasions with all kinds of prayers and requests."
> (Ephesians 6:18)

Conditions on Which Successful Prayer Depends:

▶ **Are you a child of God?** Have you sincerely received Jesus Christ as Savior and Lord of your life?

"To all who did receive him, to those who believed in his name, he gave the right to become children of God—children born not of natural descent, nor of human decision or a husband's will, but born of God" (John 1:12–13).

▶ **Have you confessed** and repented of any known sin in your life?

"If I had cherished sin in my heart, the Lord would not have listened; but God has surely listened and has heard my prayer" (Psalm 66:18–19).

▶ **Are you asking** on the basis of having worked hard for God, followed the rules, or been a "good person"? Or do you base your prayer on your relationship with the Lord Jesus Christ, on who He is and what He has done for you?

"I will do whatever you ask in my name, so that the Father may be glorified in the Son. You may ask me for anything in my name ... " (John 14:13–14).

▶ **Is your request** within the will of God?

"This is the confidence we have in approaching God: that if we ask anything according to his will, he hears us" (1 John 5:14).

▶ **Do you believe** in your heart that God has the power to provide and is willing to answer your prayer?

"I tell you, whatever you ask for in prayer, believe that you have received it, and it will be yours" (Mark 11:24).

▶ **Instead of desiring** your own will, are you willing to accept God's will with a submissive heart like Jesus did when He prayed ...

"Father ... everything is possible for you. ... Yet not what I will, but what you will" (Mark 14:36).

And are you willing to follow the instructions Paul gave the Christians at Philippi?

> "Do not be anxious about anything,
> but in every situation,
> by prayer and petition, with thanksgiving,
> present your requests to God."
> (Philippians 4:6)

QUESTION: "If I give money to God, can I expect Him to bless me with financial gain?"

ANSWER: God does not guarantee financial wealth, yet many Christians secretly "give to get." The truth is, if we want to imitate God, we need to give as He gives—unconditionally, from a loving heart for the recipient—not out of a selfish heart desiring our own gain. Helping people amass material wealth is not God's priority. Rather, He desires that we amass spiritual riches. He alone will judge and reward the true motives of those who give.

> "All a person's ways seem pure to them,
> but motives are weighed by the Lord."
> (Proverbs 16:2)

HOW TO Say "No" When You Should Not Give

At times we have all been asked to give but didn't think the Lord was leading us to say *yes* to that particular request. The dilemma then becomes how to say *no*. Although you will always be led to give, you will never be led to give to every request.

Any time you are in doubt as to what God's will is for you with regard to a request, claim the promise:

> **"If any of you lacks wisdom,
> you should ask God, who gives generously
> to all without finding fault,
> and it will be given to you.
> But when you ask,
> you must believe and not doubt ..."
> (James 1:5–6)**

▶ **Preparation steps to say "no"**

- Pray that the Spirit of God gives you His peace or a lack of peace about giving.

  Galatians 5:22 says, *"The fruit of the Spirit is love, joy, peace ... "*

- If you don't have peace, be straightforward, forthright, and brief. (Don't over explain.)

- Do not apologize; simply speak the truth in a polite way. (Apologizing gives the wrong message.)

- Breathe deeply before answering, make eye contact, and then speak slowly. (Otherwise "no" may sound stiff and abrupt.)

▶ A "no" response to a giving plea

- "Thank you for letting me know about the helpful/wonderful work this (state cause) is doing. However, I'm so heavily committed with other causes, that I cannot in good conscience undertake another." (or)

- "I have sincerely prayed about this decision and I simply don't have the peace of God about it." (or)

- "I'm not led by the Spirit of God to be involved, but I trust that He has laid it on the hearts of others to meet your needs."

The Bible says, *"The LORD gives strength to his people; the LORD blesses his people with peace"* (Psalm 29:11).

▶ A "no" response to a personal plea

For an *appropriate* request:

- "I understand your request for financial help to (repeat request). However, I am fully persuaded that I'm not the person God plans to use in this situation."

- "I love what you are doing and am committed to pray for you, but right now God is leading me to give elsewhere."

- "As much as I might want to help, He has not given me the freedom to do so. My conclusion can only be that He has someone else to bless you or that He has some other plan for you."

For an *inappropriate* request:

- "I understand your request for financial help to (repeat request). However, I can't in good conscience support you in this."

- "I care about you too much to do what I genuinely believe is wrong for you."

- "For both you and me, there's no right way to do a wrong act. And if I said 'yes' to you, I would be saying 'no' to God."

The Bible says, *"Am I now trying to win the approval of human beings, or of God? Or am I trying to please people? If I were still trying to please people, I would not be a servant of Christ"* (Galatians 1:10).

▶ **If still pressured, repeat your response**

- "As I said ... "

- With more pressure, restate your response, and then add, "I am not changing my answer. I must not go against what God is leading me to do."

- Walk away. Refuse to negotiate. (If you give in to pressure now, your "no" will not be believed in the future.)

The Bible says, *"Let your 'Yes' be 'Yes,' and your 'No,' 'No'"* (Matthew 5:37 NKJV).

With biblical principles undergirding his instruction, Dave Ramsey begins ministering on money matters in a church. Soon his life experiences begin to resonate with people outside the church walls. In 1992 he launches a radio program, The Dave Ramsey Show, which airs throughout the country and sustains an extremely loyal following.

Because he can relate to the excruciating pinch of financial pain, Dave vividly remembers the first time a caller contacted the show in tears, crying because she was going through a foreclosure. He describes it as a "wow" moment, more acutely recognizing the importance of sound financial counsel. "This is people's lives—their hope," Dave assesses. "It's tremendously satisfying to be doing work that impacts people."[28]

The truth is, sound financial counsel serves to free people from the deadly snare of debt. If you find yourself in such a snare, heed the words of Solomon, the wisest man who ever lived:

> "Free yourself, like a gazelle
> from the hand of the hunter,
> like a bird from the snare of the fowler."
> (Proverbs 6:5)

Identify your debt situation.

▶ **Make an inventory of your assets.**

- What do you own?
- What do you co-own in personal/business partnerships?
- What is the approximate value of the things you own (car, house, property, insurance policy—large items)?

▶ **Identify your income.**

- How much money do you make?
- How much time per week do you work to obtain this money?
- Do you have any money-producing investments?

▶ **Describe your debts.**

- What do you owe?
- When is it due?
- What interest rates are you paying on each debt?

▶ **Approximate your monthly bills.**

- What are your fixed expenses (rent/mortgage, utilities, phone, insurance)?
- What are your variable expenses (gasoline/transportation, food, clothing, entertainment)?
- What are your charitable expenses (church, ministries, etc.).

"Give to everyone what you owe them: If you owe taxes, pay taxes; if revenue, then revenue; if respect, then respect; if honor, then honor" (Romans 13:7).

CONSIDER YOUR LIFESTYLE.

▶ **Be introspective.**

- Why do you live the way you do? Is it for career advancement, to impress friends or family, or to live comfortably?
- Were you brought up living this way?
- How do your friends, family, and coworkers live?

▶ **Consider what you could do without.**

- Do you own expensive items that you do not really need, items with high maintenance costs after the initial purchase?
- Do you pay others to do something that you could do yourself?
- Do you eat out when you could eat less expensively at home?

▶ **Look for what you can substitute.**

- Can you substitute less expensive services for those you currently use?
- Can you substitute less expensive items for premium products you currently use?
- Can you substitute less expensive forms of entertainment, exercise, and enjoyment for those you currently use?

▶ **Reconsider gift giving.**

- Do you disregard budgets and savings plans during holidays and gift giving occasions?

- Can you give fewer and less expensive gifts?

- Do you seek God's will regarding every donation you make, or is it too hard for you to say "no" to requests?

"Be very careful, then, how you live—not as unwise but as wise" (Ephesians 5:15).

ESTABLISH FINANCIAL GOALS.

▶ **List future expenditures.**

- What future expenses do you anticipate?

- Are you looking to buy a home, pay for a daughter's wedding, or replace a vehicle?

- Do you expect to give any financial assistance to elderly parents or other family members?

▶ **Consider future career changes.**

- Are you considering going to school or starting your own business?

- Are you considering early or late retirement?

- How will these plans change your financial situation?

▶ **Prepare for family changes.**

- Are you expecting a child?

- Are children leaving the home?

- Are you financially prepared for health problems in your family?

▶ **State your future financial goals.**

- Financially, where do you want to be five years from now? Ten years from now?
- What strategies do you have for reaching your goals?
- What are your realistic expectations?

"The plans of the diligent lead to profit as surely as haste leads to poverty" (Proverbs 21:5).

TAKE ACTION WITH YOUR FINANCES.

▶ **Pay extra on your debts.**

- What debt has the highest interest rate?
- What amount of money can you pay each month on that debt?
- Can you pay off that debt through another avenue that charges less interest?

▶ **Stop feeding your debt.**

- What spending habits contribute to your debt?
- Have you stopped using credit cards and started paying cash?
- What new purchases are you making?

▶ **Change your lifestyle.**

- What monthly purchases can you do without?
- What amount of money do you spend on nonessentials?
- What expensive assets can you sell that would be financially profitable?

▶ **Establish a savings plan.**

- How much money are you setting aside for the future?

- How are you preparing for retirement and major emergencies so that you do not find yourself in debt again?

- Are you saving a set amount of money out of each paycheck or on a monthly basis?

▶ **Establish a giving plan.**

- How much should you plan to give for God's work?

- How much are you giving out of your monthly income?

- How much money are you setting aside to help those in need?

"Wisdom is a shelter as money is a shelter, but the advantage of knowledge is this: Wisdom preserves those who have it" (Ecclesiastes 7:12).

QUESTION: "What are common sense cost savers?"

ANSWER: There are as many ways to save while still spending. Some rules to go by include ...

▶ If you don't need it, don't buy it.

▶ If you can cook it, don't order it.

▶ If your public library has it, don't purchase it.

▶ If you can use an older one, don't buy a newer one.

- ▶ If you can use a cheaper one, don't buy a costly one.

- ▶ If you can't pay cash for it, don't buy it.

- ▶ If you can repair it, don't replace it.

- ▶ If you can still use it, don't get rid of it

Those who are shortsighted, who think only of satisfying today's desires but make no provision for tomorrow by spending wisely and frugally today, are sure to one day come up short. Then what will they do? The better part of wisdom is to make choices today keeping tomorrow in mind.

> **"The wise store up choice food and olive oil,
> but fools gulp theirs down."**
> **(Proverbs 21:20)**

HOW TO Properly Handle the Responsibilities of Money

Today Dave Ramsey is widely acclaimed for his financial expertise and has utilized multiple venues for dispensing it. Besides his radio show, Dave has authored numerous books, hosted conferences, and initiated Financial Peace University (a curriculum designed to teach sound money principles and to lead people out of debt).

Clearly, Dave practices the exhortation of Paul to the church at Thessalonica: *"Therefore encourage one another and build each other up, just as in fact you are doing"* (1 Thessalonians 5:11).

Dave has laid the groundwork for a debt-free lifestyle by developing what he calls "The Seven Baby Steps," based on the premise that you "get out of debt the same way you learned to walk—one step at a time."[29]

▶ **Step 1:** Deposit $1,000 to start an emergency fund.

▶ **Step 2:** Pay off all debts using the Debt Snowball (eliminating smallest debts first, then applying that payment toward the next smallest debt and so on).

▶ **Step 3:** Place three to six months of expenses in savings.

▶ **Step 4:** Invest 15% of household income into Roth IRAs and pre-tax retirement.

▶ **Step 5:** Begin a college fund for children.

▶ **Step 6:** Pay off your home early.

▶ **Step 7:** Build wealth and give accordingly!

Clearly, the proper handling of money in the home setting requires a division of responsibilities established by God and carried out by Him doing His part and you doing your part.

God's Part: Divine Ownership

▶ God owns everything, including your possessions.

"The earth is the Lord's, and everything in it ..." (Psalm 24:1).

▶ God owns all the land.

"The land must not be sold permanently, because the land is mine ... " (Leviticus 25:23).

▶ God owns the precious metals.

"'The silver is mine and the gold is mine,' declares the Lord Almighty" (Haggai 2:8).

▶ God owns the animals.

"Every animal of the forest is mine, and the cattle on a thousand hills. I know every bird in the mountains, and the insects in the fields are mine" (Psalm 50:10–12).

▶ God holds all things together.

"He is before all things, and in him all things hold together" (Colossians 1:17).

Your Part: Recognize God's Ownership

▶ **Plan:** For the next 30 days—when you first awake in the morning and just before going to sleep at night—meditate on 1 Chronicles 29:11–12.

"Yours, Lord, is the greatness and the power and the glory and the majesty and the splendor, for everything in heaven and earth is yours. Yours, Lord, is the kingdom; you are exalted as head over

all. Wealth and honor come from you; you are the ruler of all things. In your hands are strength and power to exalt and give strength to all."

▶ **Personalize:** Use personal pronouns to connect the passage to your life (For example, "You are the ruler of all my things. In your hands are strength and power to exalt and give strength to me.")

▶ **Pray:** Ask God to make you aware of His ownership.

▶ **Practice:** Acknowledge God's ownership every time you purchase an item.

Your Part: Honor His Lordship

▶ Give everything you have to Him.

"Those of you who do not give up everything you have cannot be my disciples" (Luke 14:33).

▶ Obey God's directive to give to Him your most treasured possessions.

"Take your son, your only son, whom you love— Isaac—and go to the region of Moriah. Sacrifice him there as a burnt offering on a mountain I will show you" (Genesis 22:2).

▶ Handle His money according to His instruction.

"Now a man named Ananias, together with his wife Sapphira, also sold a piece of property. With his wife's full knowledge he kept back part of the money for himself, but brought the rest and put it at the apostles' feet. Then Peter said, 'Ananias,

how is it that Satan has so filled your heart that you have lied to the Holy Spirit and have kept for yourself some of the money you received for the land?" (Acts 5:1–3).

▶ Take care of His possessions within your care.

"Since an overseer manages God's household, he must be blameless—not overbearing, not quick-tempered, not given to drunkenness, not violent, not pursuing dishonest gain" (Titus 1:7).

▶ Seek God and work wholeheartedly in His service.

"This is what Hezekiah did throughout Judah, doing what was good and right and faithful before the LORD his God. In everything that he undertook in the service of God's temple and in obedience to the law and the commands, he sought his God and worked wholeheartedly. And so he prospered" (2 Chronicles 31:20–21).

> *Money is not the ultimate end*
> *but merely a means to an end.*
> *And what is the end for the authentic*
> *Christian? To glorify God!*
> *You exist to reflect His reality as you live*
> *His life before others. In this marvelous*
> *way, the Bible has predetermined your*
> *purpose as well as your money's purpose—*
> *it's all for the glory of God!*
> *—June Hunt*

SCRIPTURES TO MEMORIZE

What does the Bible say about me if I **can be trusted with very little**?

*"Whoever **can be trusted with very little** can also be trusted with much, and whoever is dishonest with very little will also be dishonest with much. So if you have not been trustworthy in handling worldly wealth, who will trust you with true riches?"* (Luke 16:10–11)

Why am I **never satisfied with** my **income**?

*"Whoever loves money never has enough; whoever loves wealth is **never satisfied with** their **income**. This too is meaningless."* (Ecclesiates 5:10)

Why am I to **"store up treasures in heaven"**?

*"**Store up** for yourselves **treasures in heaven**, where moths and vermin do not destroy. ... For where your treasure is, there your heart will be also."* (Matthew 6:20–21)

Who **gives** me the **strength** and **ability to produce wealth**?

*"You may say to yourself, 'My power and the **strength** of my hands have produced this wealth for me.' But remember the LORD your God, for it is he who **gives** you the **ability to produce wealth** ... "* (Deuteronomy 8:17–18)

Who becomes a **slave to the lender**?

*" ... the borrower is **slave to the lender**."* (Proverbs 22:7)

To whom should I look to **meet all** my financial **needs**?

*"My God will **meet all** your **needs** according to the riches of his glory in Christ Jesus."* (Philippians 4:19)

Because **life does not consist in an abundance of possessions**, what should I **be on guard against**?

*"**Be on** your **guard against** all kinds of greed; **life does not consist in an abundance of possessions**."* (Luke 12:15)

Why can't I **serve God** and **be devoted to** Him and at the same time **love money**?

*"No one can **serve** two masters. Either you will hate the one and love the other, or you will **be devoted to** the one and despise the other. You cannot **serve** both **God** and **money**."* (Matthew 6:24)

What does the Bible say is **a root of all kinds of evil**?

*"The love of money is **a root of all kinds of evil**. Some people, eager for money, have wandered from the faith and pierced themselves with many griefs."* (1 Timothy 6:10)

What will help me to remain **free from the love of money**?

*"Keep your lives **free from the love of money** and be content with what you have, because God has said, 'Never will I leave you; never will I forsake you.'"* (Hebrews 13:5)

NOTES

1. Chris Dolmetsch, "NYC's $168 Million Lottery Winner Plans to Travel," bloomberg.com, September 15, 2009, http://www.bloomberg.com/apps/news?pid=newsarchi ve&sid=acok6MoUTSI0.

2. Deena Winter, "Financial Planners: Winning the Lottery Isn't Always a Dream," journalstar.com, February 24, 2006, http://journalstar.com/special-section/news/financial-planners-winning-the-lottery-isn-t-always-a-dream/article_ecba141b-3e59-5914-a321-38b4adb20733.html.

3. Larry Celona, Brendan Scott, Austin Fenner, Dan Mangan, "Once-Broke Harlem Man in the Money." nypost.com, September 9, 2009, http://nypost.com/2009/09/09/once-broke-harlem-man-in-the-money/.

4. *Merriam-Webster's Online Dictionary*, s.v. "Finance."

5. *Merriam-Webster,* s.v. "Money."

6. *Merriam-Webster,* s.v. "Steward."

7. *Merriam-Webster,* s.v. "Debt."

8. Ellen Goodstein, "8 Lottery Winners Who Lost Their Millions," bankrate.com, March 29, 2006, http://www.bankrate.com/brm/news/advice/20041108a1.asp.

9. Goodstein, "8 Lottery Winners"

10. Francis Brown, Samuel Rolles Driver, Charles Augustus Briggs, *Enhanced Brown-Driver-Briggs Hebrew and English Lexicon*, electronic ed. (Oak Harbor, WA : Logos Research Systems, 2000), #493.

11. *Merriam-Webster,* s.v. "Mammon."

12. Robert Horst Balz, Gerhard Schneider, *Exegetical Dictionary of the New Testament* (Grand Rapids: Eerdmans, 1993), vol. 2, 382–383.

13. James Strong, *The Exhaustive Concordance of the Bible : Showing Every Word of the Test of the Common English Version of the Canonical Books, and Every*

Occurence of Each Word in Regular Order, electronic ed. (Bellingham, WA : Logos, 1996), s.v. G#3623.

14. Strong, *The Exhaustive Concordance*, s.v. G#5533.

15. Goodstein, "8 Lottery Winners"

16. Dave and Neta Jackson, *Hero Tales* (Minneapolis: Bethany House, 1996), 107.

17. Jackson, *Hero Tales*, 107.

18. Jackson, *Hero Tales*, 107–108.

19. Jackson, *Hero Tales*, 108.

20. Jackson, *Hero Tales*, 110.

21. Jackson, *Hero Tales*, 111.

22. John Piper, "George Mueller's Strategy for Showing God," http://www.desiringgod.org/biographies/george-muellers-strategy-for-showing-god.

23. Pablo S. Torre, "How (and Why) Athletes Go Broke," *Sports Illustrated* (New York: Time Warner, March 23, 2009), http://sportsillustrated.cnn.com/vault/article/magazine/MAG1153364/1/index.htm.

24. Billy Corben, *30 for 30: Broke* (Bristol, CT: ESPN, October 2, 2012), http://espn.go.com/30for30/film?page=broke.

25. Corben, *30 for 30: Broke*

26. Lawrence J. Crabb, Jr., *Understanding People: Deep Longings for Relationship*, Ministry Resources Library (Grand Rapids: Zondervan, 1987), 15–16; Robert S. McGee, *The Search for Significance*, 2nd ed. (Houston, TX: Rapha, 1990), 27–30.

27. Dave Ramsey, "Who Do You Trust?" daveramsey.com, April 22, 2010, http://www.daveramsey.com/article/who-do-you-trust/lifeandmoney_bankruptcy/.

28. Carole Robinson, "The Dave Ramsey Show Celebrates 20 Years" *Williamson Herald*, September 26, 2012.

29. Dave Ramsey, "The Seven Baby Steps" (Brentwood, TN: The Lampo Group, 2014), http://www.daveramsey.com/new/baby-steps/.

HOPE FOR THE HEART TITLES

- *Adultery*
- *Aging Well*
- *Alcohol & Drug Abuse*
- *Anger*
- *Anorexia & Bulimia*
- *Boundaries*
- *Bullying*
- *Caregiving*
- *Chronic Illness & Disability*
- *Codependency*
- *Conflict Resolution*
- *Confrontation*
- *Considering Marriage*
- *Critical Spirit*
- *Decision Making*
- *Depression*
- *Domestic Violence*
- *Dysfunctional Family*
- *Envy & Jealousy*
- *Fear*
- *Financial Freedom*
- *Forgiveness*
- *Friendship*
- *Gambling*
- *Grief*
- *Guilt*
- *Hope*
- *Loneliness*
- *Manipulation*
- *Marriage*
- *Overeating*
- *Parenting*
- *Perfectionism*
- *Procrastination*
- *Reconciliation*
- *Rejection*
- *Self-Worth*
- *Sexual Integrity*
- *Singleness*
- *Spiritual Abuse*
- *Stress*
- *Success Through Failure*
- *Suicide Prevention*
- *Trials*
- *Verbal & Emotional Abuse*
- *Victimization*

www.hendricksonrose.com